D0205978

The Evolution of the International Economic Order

The Eliot Janeway Lectures
on Historical Economics
in Honor of
JOSEPH SCHUMPETER
Princeton University
1977

The Evolution of the International Economic Order

W. Arthur Lewis

PRINCETON UNIVERSITY PRESS

Published by Princeton University Press,
Princeton, New Jersey

In the United Kingdom: Princeton University Press,
Guildford, Surrey

Library of Congress Cataloging in Publication Data will
be found on the last printed page of this book

This book has been composed in VIP Bembo

Printed in the United States of America
by Princeton University Press, Princeton, New Jersey

Designed by Laury A. Egan

CONTENTS

PREFACE

This is the substance of two public lectures delivered at Princeton University on March 15 and 16, 1977. The material is slightly expanded here, but the lecture style is retained. As delivered, the lectures came to no conclusions; I have added a brief postscript to clarify my own stance.

The Janeway Lectures are an annual series initiated by Eliot and Elizabeth Janeway in honour of Joseph Schumpeter, who was Professor of Economics at Harvard University from 1932 to 1950. Schumpeter's writings are distinguished by his felicitous combination of history, economics, and statistics, and the lectures are intended to help preserve this tradition. It is a great honour to be chosen to walk in these footsteps.

W. A. L.

The
Evolution
of the
International
Economic
Order

INTRODUCTION

In international circles the topic of the day is the demand of the Third World for a new international economic order. My topic is the evolution of the existing economic order: how it came into existence not much more than a century ago, and how it has been changing.

The phrase "international economic order" is vague, but nothing would be gained by trying to define it precisely. I will discuss certain elements of the relationship between the developing and the developed countries that the developing countries find particularly irksome. These are:

First, the division of the world into exporters of primary products and exporters of manufactures.

Second, the adverse factoral terms of trade for the products of the developing countries.

Third, the dependence of the developing countries on the developed for finance.

Fourth, the dependence of the developing countries on the developed for their engine of growth.

My purpose in treating these topics is not to make recommendations, but to try to understand how we come to be where we are.

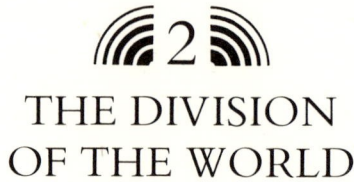

THE DIVISION
OF THE WORLD

How did the world come to be divided into industrial countries and agricultural countries? Did this result from geographical resources, economic forces, military forces, some international conspiracy, or what?

In talking about industrialization, we are talking about very recent times. England has seen many industrial revolutions since the thirteenth century, but the one that changed the world began at the end of the eighteenth century. It crossed rapidly to North America and to Western Europe, but even as late as 1850 it had not matured all that much. In 1850 Britain was the only country in the world where the agricultural population had fallen below 50 percent of the labor force. Today some 30 Third World countries already have agricultural populations equal to less than 50 percent of the labor force—17 in Latin America, 8 in Asia not including Japan, and 5 in Africa not counting South Africa. Thus, except for Britain, even the oldest of the industrial countries were in only the early stages of structural transformation in 1850.

At the end of the eighteenth century, trade between what are now the industrial countries and what is now the Third World was based on geography rather than on structure; indeed India was the leading exporter of fine cotton fabrics. The trade was also trivially small in volume. It consisted of sugar, a few spices, precious metals, and luxury goods. It was then cloaked in much romance, and had caused much bloodshed, but it simply did not amount to much.

In the course of the first half of the nineteenth century industrialization changed the composition of the trade, since Britain captured world trade in iron and in cotton fabrics; but the volume of trade with the Third World continued to be small. Even as late as 1883, the first year for which we have a calculation, total imports into the United States and Western Europe from Asia, Africa, and tropical Latin America came only to about a dollar per head of the population of the exporting countries.★

There are two reasons for this low volume of trade. One is that the leading industrial countries—Britain, the United States, France, and Germany—were, taken together, virtually self-sufficient. The raw materials of the industrial revolution were coal, iron ore, cotton, and wool, and the foodstuff was wheat. Between them, these core countries had all they needed except for wool. Although many writers have stated that the industrial revolution depended on the raw materials of the Third World, this is quite untrue. Not until what is

★ For the sources of this and other statistics used here, and generally for more detailed historical analysis, the reader may consult my book, *Growth and Fluctuations 1870-1913*, Allen and Unwin, London 1978.

sometimes called the second industrial revolution, at the end of the nineteenth century (Schumpeter's Third Kondratiev upswing based on electricity, the motor car and so on), did a big demand for rubber, copper, oil, bauxite, and such materials occur. The Third World's contribution to the industrial revolution of the first half of the nineteenth century was negligible.

The second reason why trade was so small is that the expansion of world trade, which created the international economic order that we are considering, is necessarily an offshoot of the transport revolutions. In this case, the railway was the major element. Before the railway the external trade of Africa or Asia or Latin America was virtually though not completely confined to the seacoasts and rivers; the railway altered this. Although the industrial countries were building railways from 1830 on, the railway did not reach the Third World until the 1860s. The principal reason for this was that, in most countries, railways were financed by borrowing in London—even the North American railways were financed in London—and the Third World did not begin to borrow substantially in London until after 1860. The other revolution in transport was the decline in ocean freights, which followed the substitution of iron for wooden hulls and of steam for sails. Freights began to fall after the middle of the century, but their spectacular downturn came after 1870, when they fell by two-thirds over thirty years.

For all these reasons, the phenomenon we are

exploring—the entry of the tropical countries significantly into world trade—really belongs only to the last quarter of the nineteenth century. It is then that tropical trade began to grow significantly—at about four percent a year in volume. And it is then that the international order that we know today established itself.

Now it is not obvious why the tropics reacted to the industrial revolution by becoming exporters of agricultural products.

As the industrial revolution developed in the leading countries in the first half of the nineteenth century it challenged the rest of the world in two ways. One challenge was to imitate it. The other challenge was to trade. As we have just seen, the trade opportunity was small and was delayed until late in the nineteenth century. But the challenge to imitate and have one's own industrial revolution was immediate. In North America and in Western Europe, a number of countries reacted immediately. Most countries, however, did not, even in Central Europe. This was the point at which the world began to divide into industrial and non-industrial countries.

Why did it happen this way? The example of industrialization would have been easy to follow. The industrial revolution started with the introduction of new technologies in making textiles, mining coal, smelting pig iron, and using steam. The new ideas were ingenious but simple and easy to apply. The capital requirement was remarkably small, except for the cost of building railways, which could be had on loan. There were no great economies of scale, so the skills required for managing a factory or workshop were well within the competence and experience of what we now call the Third World. The technology was available to any country that wanted it, despite feeble British efforts to restrict the export of machinery (which ceased after 1850), and Englishmen and Frenchmen were willing to travel to the ends of the earth to set up and operate the new mills.

Example was reinforced by what we now call "backwash." A number of Third World countries were exporting manufactures in 1800, notably India. Cheap British exports of textiles and of iron destroyed such trade, and provided these countries an incentive to adopt the new British techniques. India built its first modern textile mill in 1853, and by the end of the century was not only self-sufficient in the cheaper cottons, but had also driven British yarn out of many Far Eastern markets. Why then did not the whole world immediately adopt the techniques of the industrial revolution?

The favorite answer to this question is political, but it will not wash. It is true that imperial powers were hostile to industrialization in their colonies. The British tried to stop the cotton industry in India by taxing it. They failed because the Indian cotton industry had the protection of lower wages and of lower transportation costs. But they did succeed in holding off iron and steel production in India till as late as 1912. The hostility of imperial powers to industrialization in their colonies and in the "open door" countries is beyond dispute. But the world was not all colonial in the middle of the nineteenth century. When the coffee industry began to expand rapidly in Brazil around 1850, there was no external political force from Europe or North America that made Brazil develop as a coffee exporter instead of as an industrial nation. Brazil, Argentina, and all the rest of Latin America were free to industrialize, but did not. India, Ceylon, Java, and the Philippines were colonies, but in 1850 there were still no signs of industrialization in Thailand or Japan or China, Indo-China or the rest of the Indonesian archipelago. The partition of Africa did not come until 1880, when the industrial revolution was already a hundred years old. We cannot escape the fact that Eastern and Southern Europe were just as backward in industrializing as South Asia or Latin America. Political independence alone is an insufficient basis for industrialization.

We must therefore turn to economic explanations. The most important of these, and the most neglected, is the dependence of an industrial revolution on a prior or simultaneous agricultural revolution. This argument was already familiar to eighteenth-century economists, including Sir James Steuart and Adam Smith.

In a closed economy, the size of the industrial sector is a function of agricultural productivity. Agriculture has to be capable of producing the surplus food and raw materials consumed in the industrial sector, and it is the affluent state of the farmers that enables them to be a market for industrial products. If the domestic market is too small, it is still possible to support an industrial sector by exporting manufactures and importing food and raw materials. But it is hard to begin industrialization by exporting manufactures. Usually one begins by selling in a familiar and protected home market and moves on to exporting only after one has learnt to make one's costs competitive.

The distinguishing feature of the industrial revolution at the end of the eighteenth century is that it began in the country with the highest agricultural productivity—Great Britain—which therefore already had a large industrial sector. The industrial revolution did not create an industrial sector where none had been before. It transformed an industrial sector that already existed by introducing new ways of making the same old things. The revolution spread rapidly in other countries that were also revolutionizing their agriculture, especially in Western Europe and North America. But countries of low agricultural productivity, such as Central and Southern Europe, or Latin America, or China had rather small industrial sectors, and there it made rather slow progress.

If the smallness of the market was one constraint on industrialization, because of low agricultural productivity, the absence of an investment climate was another. Western Europe had been creating a capitalist environment for at least a century; thus a whole new set of people, ideas and institutions was established that did not exist in Asia or Africa, or even for the most part in Latin America, despite the closer cultural heritage. Power in these countries—as also in Central and Southern Europe—was still concentrated in the hands of landed classes, who benefited from cheap imports and saw no reason to support the emergence of a new industrial class. There was no industrial entrepreneurship. Of course the agricultural countries were just as capable of sprouting an industrial complex of skills, institutions, and ideas, but this would take time. In the meantime it was relatively easy for them to respond to the other opportunity the industrial revolution now opened up, namely to export agricultural products, especially as transport costs came down. There was no lack of traders to travel through the countryside collecting small parcels of produce from thousands of small farmers, or of landowners, domestic or foreign, ready to man plantations with imported Indian or Chinese labor.

And so the world divided: countries that industrialized and exported manufactures, and the other countries that exported agricultural products. The speed of this adjustment, especially in the second half of the nineteenth century, created an illusion. It came to be an article of faith in Western Europe that the tropical countries had a comparative advantage in agriculture. In fact, as Indian textile production soon began to show, between the tropical and temperate countries, the differences in food production per head were much greater than in modern industrial production per head.

Now we come to another problem. I stated earlier that the industrial revolution presented two alternative challenges—an opportunity to industrialize by example and an opportunity to trade. But an opportunity to trade is also an opportunity to industrialize. For trade increases the national income, and therefore increases the domestic market for manufactures. Import substitution becomes possible, and industrialization can start off from there. This for example is what happened to Australia, whose development did not begin until the gold rush of the 1850s, and was then based on exporting primary products. Nevertheless by 1913 the proportion of Australia's labor force in agriculture had fallen to 25 percent, and Australia was producing more manufactures per head than France or Germany. Why did this not happen to all the other agricultural countries?

The absence of industrialization in these countries was not due to any failure of international trade to expand. The volume of trade of the tropical countries increased at a rate of about 4 percent per annum over the thirty years before the first world war. So if trade was the engine of growth of the tropics, and industry the engine of growth of the industrial countries, we can say that the tropical engine was beating as fast as the industrial engine. The relative failure of India tends to overshadow developments elsewhere, but countries such as Ceylon, Thailand, Burma, Brazil, Colombia, Ghana, or Uganda were transformed during these thirty years before the First World War. They built themselves roads, schools, water supplies, and other essential infrastructure. But they did not become industrial nations.

There are several reasons for this, of which the most important is their terms of trade. Thus, we must spend a little time analyzing what determined the terms of trade.

THE FACTORAL TERMS
OF TRADE

The development of the agricultural countries in the second half of the nineteenth century was promoted by two vast streams of international migration. About fifty million people left Europe for the temperate settlements, of whom about thirteen million went to what we now call the new countries of temperate settlement: Canada, Argentina, Chile, Australia, New Zealand, and South Africa. About the same number—fifty million people—left India and China to work mainly as indentured laborers in the tropics on plantations, in mines, or in construction projects. The availability of these two streams set the terms of trade for tropical and temperate agricultural commodities, respectively. For temperate commodities the market forces set prices that could attract European migrants, while for tropical commodities they set prices that would sustain indentured Indians. These were very different levels.

A central cause of this difference was the difference in agricultural productivity between Europe and the tropics. In Britain, which was the biggest single source of European migration, the yield of wheat by 1900 was 1,600 lbs. per acre, as against the tropical yield of 700 lbs. of grain per acre. The

European also had better equipment and cultivated more acres per man, so the yield per man must have been six or seven times larger than in tropical regions. Also, in the country to which most of the European migrants went (the United States), the yield differential was even higher, not because of productivity per acre, which was lower than in Europe, but because of greater mechanization. The new temperate settlements could attract and hold European immigrants, in competition with the United States, only by offering income levels higher than prevailed in Northwest Europe. Since Northwest Europe needed first their wool, and then after 1890 their frozen meat, and ultimately after 1900 their wheat, it had to pay for those commodities prices that would yield a higher-than-European standard of living.

In the tropical situation, on the other hand, any prices for tea or rubber or peanuts that would offer a standard of living in excess of the 700 lb. of grain per acre level were an improvement. Farmers would consider devoting idle land or time to producing such crops; as their experience grew, they would even, at somewhat higher prices, reduce their own subsistence production of food in order to specialize in commercial crops. But regardless of how the small farmer reacted, there was an unlimited supply of Indians and Chinese willing to travel anywhere to work on plantations for a shilling a day. This stream of migrants from Asia was as large as the stream from Europe and set the level of tropical prices. In the 1880s the wage of a plantation laborer was one shilling a day, but the wage of an unskilled construction worker in Australia was nine shillings a day. If tea had been a temperate instead of a tropical crop, its price would have been perhaps four times as high as it was. And if wool had been a tropical instead of a temperate crop, it could have been had for perhaps one-fourth of the ruling price.

This analysis clearly turns on the long-run infinite elasticity of the supply of labor to any one activity at prices determined by farm productivity in Europe and Asia, respectively. This is applied to a Ricardian-type comparative cost model with two countries and three goods. The fact that one of these goods, food, is produced by both countries determines the factoral terms of trade, in terms of food. As usual one can elaborate by increasing the number of goods or countries, but the essence remains if food production is common to all.

One important conclusion is that the tropical countries cannot escape from these unfavorable terms of trade by increasing productivity in the commodities they export, since this will simply reduce the prices of such commodities. Indeed we have seen this quite clearly in the two commodities in which productivity has risen most, sugar and rubber. The factoral terms of trade can be improved only by raising tropical productivity in the common commodity, domestic foodstuffs.

There are interesting borderline cases where the two groups of countries compete. Cotton is an example. In the nineteenth century, the United

States was the principal supplier of cotton, but the crop could also grow all over the tropics. The United States maintained its hold on the market despite eager British efforts to promote cotton growing in the British colonies. The U.S. yields per acre were about three times as high as the Indian or African yields, but this alone would not have been enough to discourage tropical production. The United States could not have competed with tropical cotton had southern blacks been free to migrate to the North and to work there at white Northern incomes. It was racial discrimination in the United States that kept the price of cotton so low; or, to turn this around, given the racial discrimination, American blacks earned so little because of the large amount of cotton that would have flowed out of Asia and Africa and Latin America at a higher cotton price.

Cotton was one of a set of commodities where low agricultural productivity excluded tropical competition. The tropics could compete in any commodity where the difference in wages exceeded the difference in productivity. This ruled out not only cotton and tobacco, which fell to the ex-slaves in North America, but also maize, beef, and timber, for which there were buoyant markets, and ground was lost steadily in sugar as beet productivity increased. This left a rather narrow range of agricultural exports and contributed to the over-specialization of each tropical country in one or sometimes two export crops. Low productivity in food set the factoral terms of trade, while relative productivity in other agriculture determined which crops were in and which were out.

Minerals fall into this competing set. Labor could be had very cheaply in the tropical countries, so high productivity yielded high rents. These rents accrued to investors to whom governments had given mining concessions for next to nothing, and the proceeds flowed overseas as dividends. Mineral-bearing lands were not infinitely elastic, but the labor force was. With the arrival of colonial independence over the last two decades, the struggle of the newly independent nations to recapture for the domestic revenues the true value of the minerals in the ground, whether by differential taxation, by differential wages for miners, or by expropriation, has been one of the more bitter aspects of the international confrontation.

Given this difference in the factoral terms of trade, the opportunity that international trade presented to the new temperate settlements was very different from the opportunity presented to the tropics. Trade offered the temperate settlements high income per head, from which would immediately ensue a large demand for manufactures, opportunities for import substitution, and rapid urbanization. Domestic saving per head would be large. Money would be available to spend on schools, at all levels, and soon these countries would have a substantial managerial and administrative elite. These new temperate countries would thus create their own power centers, with money, education, and managerial capacity, independent of and somewhat hostile to the imperial power. Thus, Australia, New Zealand, and Canada ceased to be colonies in any political sense long before they acquired formal rights of sovereignty, and had already set up barriers to imports from Britain. The factoral terms available to them offered them the opportunity for full development in every sense of the word.

The factoral terms available to the tropics, on the other hand, offered the opportunity to stay poor—at any rate until such time as the labor reservoirs of India and China might be exhausted. A farmer in Nigeria might tend his peanuts with as much diligence and skill as a farmer in Australia tended his sheep, but the return would be very different. The just price, to use the medieval term, would have rewarded equal competence with equal earnings. But the market price gave the Nigerian for his peanuts a 700-lbs.-of-grain-per-acre level of living, and the Australian for his wool a 1600-lbs.-per-acre level of living, not because of differences in competence, nor because of marginal utilities or productivities in peanuts or wool, but because these were the respective amounts of food that their cousins could produce on the family farms. This is the fundamental sense in which the leaders of the less developed world denounce the current international economic order as unjust, namely that the factoral terms of trade are based on the market forces of opportunity cost and not on the just principle of equal pay for equal work. And of course nobody understood this mechanism bet-

ter than the working classes in the temperate settlements themselves, and in the United States. The
working classes were always adamant against Indian or Chinese immigration into their countries
because they realized that, if unchecked, it would
drive wages down close to Indian and Chinese
levels.★

★ I have borrowed passages from my paper "The Diffusion
of Development" in Thomas Wilson, Editor, *The Market and
the State*, Oxford University Press, Oxford 1976.

CUMULATIVE FORCES

Now let me come to more recent developments. I must first make the point that, in spite of the poor factoral terms of trade, the opportunity to trade did substantially raise the national incomes of those tropical countries that participated in trade. This was partly because prices had to be set at levels that would bring the produce out. So, although prices were based on the low productivity in food, they had to be set somewhat higher. Just as wages were higher in Australia and Argentina than in Paris or London, so also wages were higher in Ceylon or Burma than in India or China.

The other reason national incomes of some tropical countries increased was that these countries developed by bringing unused resources into use—both unused land and unused labor—so that to a large extent what they produced for export was additional to what they would otherwise have produced. In particular the tropical countries continued to be self-sufficient in food. The agricultural exports were extra output.

This steady increase in income over some sixty or seventy years, right down to the great depression of 1929, very considerably expanded the demand for manufactures. Imports of textiles and of iron goods mounted, putting domestic handicrafts out of business. Why did not these countries set up their own modern factories to cope with this rising demand?

Some did—especially India, Ceylon, Brazil, and Mexico—but progress was slow. Apart from colonialism, which restricted some but not others, three other factors worked against industrialization.

The first reason is that to a large extent the import and export trades of these countries were controlled by foreign hands. This was where the profits were, in a complex of wholesaling, banking, shipping, and insurance. Railway, plantation, and mining profits were much more volatile. Profits provide a major source of funds for reinvestment. Had trading profits accumulated in domestic hands, there would have been more domestic reinvestment, and almost certainly more interest in domestic manufacturing.

Foreigners participated heavily in the external trade of these countries for a variety of economic, cultural, and political reasons. On the economic side there was advantage in large scale operations because they minimized the usual riskiness of trading and avoided the possibility facing small traders, who could be wiped out by a bad season. On the cultural side Europeans had been running big shipping and trading enterprises since the seventeenth century; in this as also in banking and insurance, they had a considerable lead over Latin Americans and Africans, though not over Indians or Chinese. The political factor was a further complication in that some imperial governments deliberately favored their nationals at the expense both of indigenous and of other foreign competitors. Whatever the reason, the points where profits were greatest (wholesaling, banking, shipping, insurance) tended to be foreign-controlled, and this certainly diminished the availability of funds and enterprise for investment in domestic manufacturing.

A second factor to which some nationalist historians attach much importance is the fact that participation in trade itself whets the appetite for foreign goods, in the process destroying local industry. The consumer learns to prefer wheat to yams and cement to local building materials. This is all right if the country has the raw materials and can acquire the new skills for processing them. Otherwise it reduces the export multiplier—the extent to which the proceeds of exports circulate within the country, stimulating domestic industry, before flowing out again. It is difficult to give this quantitative significance for the nineteenth century, since the products destroyed by imports from Britain were mostly cotton and iron manufactures not essentially different from the imports which replaced them. Some of the difference lay in consumer preference, but most of the difference lay in cost. The situation evolved differently in the twentieth century when brand names established their footing in many consumer markets and proved difficult to dislodge even with domestic products of equal cost and quality.

As long ago as 1841, Friederich List emphasized

that the market forces in an agricultural economy work to keep it agricultural unless special measures are taken to arrest their momentum and change their direction. List's remedy was for the government to protect an infant manufacturing industry with tariffs and quotas. But this presupposes that the industrial forces have already conquered the government and can use it to their advantage. The fact that they had not is the third explanation why the agricultural countries, though becoming more prosperous and consuming more and more manufactures, did not industrialize. Imperial power was of course an obstacle in the colonial countries, but is not a necessary explanation since the same happened in the independent countries. The fact is that the very success of the country in exporting created a vested interest of those who lived by primary production—small farmers no less than big capitalists—and who opposed measures for industrialization, whether because such measures might deflect resources from agriculture and raise factor prices, or because they might result in raising the prices of manufactured goods. The outcome therefore depended on the relative political strengths of the industrial and the agricultural interests.

It is not to be supposed that in this confrontation the entrenched agricultural forces always won. On the contrary, they lost in most European countries and in most of the countries of new settlement. In Latin America at the end of the century the liveliness of Brazilian and Mexican entrepreneurs is notable. Egypt contrasts with India in not producing a single industrialist from its prosperous landowning and merchant classes. To unravel the different responses of countries experiencing apparently similar forces is a source of historical excitement. The contrast between Argentina and Australia is particularly instructive. These two countries began to grow rapidly at the same time, the 1850s, and sold the same commodities—cereals, wool, and meat. In 1913 their incomes per head were among the world's top ten. But Australia industrialized rapidly, and Argentina did not, a failure which cost her dearly after the war when the terms of trade moved against agriculture. Some Argentinian nationalists blame this failure on British interests in Argentina, but the British had even more influence in Australia or Canada, which were industrializing rapidly. The crucial difference between the two countries was that Argentinian politics were dominated by an old, landed aristocracy. Australia had no landed aristocracy. Its politics were dominated by its urban communities, who used their power to protect industrial profits and wages. The slowness with which industrial classes emerged in Latin America, or Central Europe, North Africa or much of Asia is explained as much by internal social and political structure as by the impact of external forces.

COMMODITY POLICY

The year 1929 was a turning point in the international economy: the start of the greatest depression the world has seen in the last two centuries. This great depression played havoc with the tropical countries and gave force to two movements that are still reverberating—the quest for international commodity agreements and industrialization for import substitution.

The commodity terms of trade moved sharply against agriculture in the 1930s. The price of tropical crops is tied to the price of food, through substitution possibilities; but the price of food in terms of manufactures is in practice determined mainly by acceleration or deceleration of U.S. farm output. It is sometimes alleged that agriculture's terms of trade have been moving downward continually since 1880, but this is not so. There are long swings in the terms of trade, associated with changes in the relative growth rates of industry and agriculture. The terms of trade moved against agriculture in the 1880s and 1890s, then moved rapidly in favor of agriculture down to the First World War. That period of about twenty years is remarkably like our own. U.S. agriculture had grown rapidly after the Civil War, but from the late 1890s it slowed to a more moderate pace. Food prices rose between 1900 and the war, producing a general inflation of prices. We heard the same cries then as we hear today that the world was headed towards famine. After the war, however, the terms of trade turned against agriculture through the 1920s and 1930s. They moved up in the 1940s, moved down in the 1950s and 1960s, and have moved up again since about 1970. This forty-year cycle has been with us for a century and a half, though whether it will continue nobody can predict.

International commodity agreements date back to the 1920s and were fairly numerous in the 1930s. The crux of any attempt to use them to raise prices above the market level is the ability to control supplies. Brazil's effort to maintain coffee prices dates back to its valorization scheme of 1906, and is one of the reasons why the supply of coffee has grown so rapidly in other countries. The international tea agreement, promoted by Asian suppliers, led to increasing supplies from Africa. And so on. To increase prices of agricultural commodities when one cannot control new planting is self-defeating.

Unfortunately for the developing countries, the number of commodities whose supplies can be effectively controlled is rather small.

Recognition of this factor led the developing countries to try a new tactic after the Second World War. They agreed, in line with United Nations discussions, that an international commodity agreement should not be signed by producing countries only, as was generally the case before the war, but would instead be negotiated and signed jointly by producing and consuming countries. This requirement obviously constrained the freedom of producing countries to select the price targets of the agreement. They hoped, however, that the consuming countries would lend strength to the agreement by agreeing to police supplies, e.g., by refusing to import from countries not signatory to the agreement or by refusing supplies from countries exceeding their quotas.

In the event, most international commodity negotiations have broken down on prices. Consumer and producer nations have not been able to reach agreement. The agreement of 1973 between the oil producers to raise oil prices is a return to the prewar mode. The consumers are not a party to the agreement, and are not consulted.

Interest in commodity schemes comes and goes. The less developed countries (or LDCs) are hot for commodity agreements when prices are on the long downswing, as they were in the 1950s and 1960s. When the long upswing returns it is the turn of the industrial countries to worry. True to form, last year at the U.N. Conference on Trade and Development (UNCTAD) in Nairobi, Dr. Kissinger proposed to set up a large fund to invest in increasing the output of raw materials. He would not accept the proposal for buffer stocks, but President Carter has done so more recently, bringing the United States into line with the Europeans, who had already done so. The combination of buffer stocks with a large increase in the output of commodities would suit the more developed countries very well, but it is not quite what the LDCs had in mind. On this stage the actors are liable to change their roles as the play proceeds.

Producing countries could get around their inability to control supplies if they agreed among themselves not on a target price nor on individual quotas but simply on an export tax that they would all levy. This would in time raise their receipts without raising the price received by the producing firms or farmers. Thus the country would gain more revenue without simultaneously giving producers any incentive to produce more. It should not be any more difficult to get producer agreement to an export tax than to an agreement on prices and quotas. (Such a tax would be applied only to commodities for which the demand is inelastic, but the same limitation governs any commodity scheme.)

The foregoing remarks relate to attempts to use commodity agreements as a means of turning the terms of trade in favor of the developing countries. Current discussion refers to "price stabilization" and "indexing," and therefore implies that the intention is not to raise the terms of trade, but to keep them constant. If this is so, the problem of controlling supplies does not arise.

Many Keynesian economists have advocated international commodity price stabilization, whether in the form of a commodity reserve currency, or in the form of international buffer stocks, in order to help maintain international purchasing power on the onset of a recession. A mechanism of this kind would do as much for the developed countries as for the developing, since it would help the developed to maintain their exports and therefore their employment levels. Given that all parties stand to gain, we may expect some progress in this area, though it is bound to be delayed by disagreement on price levels.

THE RISE
OF MANUFACTURING

A second change has taken place since 1929. The great depression moved the commodity terms of trade against the tropical countries, and also dried up the demand for their exports. As their purchasing power fell, money for imports vanished. So the depression gave a direct fillip to industrialization for import substitution, especially in Latin America. Even more important, it broke the back of the political resistance to industrialization— whether it had been the resistance of imperial powers or the resistance of domestic vested interests in primary production.

After the Second World War the tropical countries plunged into import substitution. Rapid progress was made in the 1950s and 1960s. Industrial production in these countries grew at about 6½ percent per annum, which compares to the 5½ percent growth rate in the developed countries.

However, by the end of the 1960s the early starters were already reaching the limits of import substitution, and industrialization began to slow down. I began this book by referring to the dependence of an industrial revolution on a prior or simultaneous agricultural revolution. If 70 percent of the labor force consists of low productivity food farmers, with only a tiny surplus, the market for domestic manufactures is strictly limited. As the limits are approached, the pace of industrialization can be maintained only by exporting manufactures.

This is indeed what has happened. The tropical countries have burst into exporting manufactures to one another, but even more to the developed countries. Their volume of exports has been growing at the extraordinary rate of 10 percent per annum. A large segment of the current discussion of a new international economic order is concerned with reducing the barriers and widening the market for the manufactures of developing countries, to be imported into developed countries.

This involves such a major reshaping of the international economic order as we have known it that we must spend a moment examining how it has come about.

In the past, the developed countries have gone to extremes to keep out manufactures from the developing countries, for exactly the same reason that they have kept out Asian migrants. They have imported raw produce, but have placed heavy import duties or prohibitions on refined produce in order to protect their own manufacturing capacity. Why then are they changing now?

The background to this change is the extraordinary and unexpected explosion of world production and trade since the Second World War. The world economy has developed just about twice as fast as anybody expected in 1950. In the preceding golden age of capitalism, which ran from around 1850 to 1913, output per head grew, even in the most advanced countries, by not more than 1½ to 2 percent a year. But between 1950 and 1973, output per head in the same countries grew by 3 to 4 percent per year. World trade expanded in the earlier period at 3½ to 4 percent, and in the later period at 7 to 8 percent in constant prices. Output in the developing countries also has grown about twice as fast as people thought possible in 1950.

Equally remarkable has been the absence between 1950 and 1974 of those international recessions that used to plague the world about once every eight or nine years. Most of these were relatively mild, but every second or third would prove to be a great depression, such as those of 1873, 1892, 1907, and 1929, or the latest arrival, that of 1974. The international recession of 1974 has all the marks of its predecessors, except that it is much milder. One characteristic it shares with them is its effect on economic prophecy. Starting with Marx in 1848, every time there has been a great depression, people have predicted the imminent collapse of the capitalist system, much as the early Christians were always poised for the imminent arrival of Judgment Day. So far the system has always revived and continued on its way as vigorously as before—though we have no assurance that it will always do so. Today our journals and newspapers predict that the prosperity of 1950 to 1974 will prove to have been a flash in the pan, and that we are now set on a long downward course. This remains to be seen, and the outcome will be crucial to the relations between developed and developing countries.

In the industrial countries, the combination of full employment and zero population growth produced structural changes in their labor markets, which have altered their attitudes to importing manufactures from low-wage countries.

To understand this, we have to start with the structure of their labor markets. In pure models of the market economy, labor of equal competence receives equal wages in all industries or occupations. This is not so in the real world, where there are protected jobs and low-wage jobs. Sometimes the difference is between industries; unskilled labor is paid more in, say, the motor industry than in the hospital industry. Sometimes it is between occupations; some kinds of skilled workers, e.g., printers, are able to keep their wages higher than those of persons in other occupations requiring the same degree of learning ability. Sometimes the distinction is between people of different races or sexes or religions.

We call this a "dual" or "two-sector" labor market because the natural tendency of a market economy to reach an equilibrium in which equal competence receives equal wages is arrested. Employers of workers in protected jobs would no doubt prefer to be hiring at lower wages from the low-wage sector, but they are prohibited from doing so by trade unions, by the racial, religious, or sexist prejudices of some of their irreplaceable staff, by legislation, or even merely by custom.

In an economy which is developing rapidly, the number of protected jobs, especially in manufacturing and in high-level services, grows faster than the labor force. Consequently, people are recruited into the high-wage sector from or at the expense of the low-wage sector. This puts pressure on the low-wage market, creating a shortage of unskilled labor, and threatening to raise wages. After the Second World War, the combination of near-zero population growth and unprecedented industrial growth drained Europe's resources of surplus or low wage labor. The agricultural labor force declined swiftly. There were fewer small shopkeepers and trucking firms. Western Europe ran short of nurses, police, bus conductors, unskilled factory workers, and unskilled service workers (hotel staff, hospital staff, domestic workers).

The economic system reacts to this pressure in one of four ways. The first is to pull more women into the labor force. The next is to mechanize or reorganize the low-wage jobs so that less labor is required. The third solution is a vast immigration of low-wage labor from other countries—which took millions into Western Europe from Southern Europe, Asia, and the Caribbean. This is not popular, and is not likely to revive. Failing this, the next best solution is to import low-wage manufactures from the less developed countries, and free one's own unskilled labor for work in the more productive sectors of the economy.

So in the 1960s the international economy began to turn on its head. The industrial countries invested capital in the poorer countries to produce manufactures for export. Manufactures became the fastest growing export of developing countries, growing at about 10 percent a year, or slightly faster than manufactures exported by developed countries. By 1975 manufactures were already 33 percent of the exports of the developing countries, excluding the oil countries, and if current trends continue, by 1985 more than half the exports of developing countries will be manufactures. To several LDCs the abolition of restrictions on manufactured imports is much more important than anything that can happen in the commodities area.

Also turning the international economy onto its head is what is happening in agricultural trade. With the population explosion and continued low productivity in food, the developing countries have become net importers of food, and, if current trends continue, will soon be importing more agricultural products than they export. The division of the world into developing countries that export agricultural products and import manufactures and developed countries that do the reverse is on the verge of ending.

The ending of this division exposes the fallacy of the belief that the division was based on unfavorable terms of trade for agriculture as against industry. If 60 percent of the tropical labor force is in low-productivity food, the rest of the labor force will get low prices whether it exports agricultural or industrial products. The opening of developed country markets to imports from the tropics merely opens up a new low-wage tropical export.

It is not true that the terms of trade are bad for all agriculture. Australia, New Zealand, Denmark, and others have become some of the richest countries in the world by exporting agricultural products. The terms of trade are bad only for tropical products, whether agricultural or industrial, and are bad because the market pays tropical unskilled labor, whatever it may be producing, a wage that is based on an unlimited reservoir of low-productivity food producers.

The remedy follows. The way to create a new international order is to eliminate the 50 to 60 percent of low-productivity workers in food by transforming their productivity. This would change the factoral terms of tropical trade and raise the prices of the traditional agricultural exports. It would also create an agricultural surplus that would support industrial production for the home market. These countries would then be less dependent on the rest of the world for finance or for their engine of growth, two aspects of the subject to which I now turn.

FINANCIAL DEPENDENCE

Europe has been a center of international finance for several centuries, as the Italians, the Dutch, and the British followed in each other's footsteps. Britain assumed the mantle of chief purveyor immediately after the Napoleonic war, but after a disastrous flurry with lending to Latin America in the 1820s, concentrated for the next three decades on Europe and North America, and did not lend significant sums to what is now the Third World until after the creation of the Indian Empire in 1857. Thereafter Britain was joined by France and Germany, and at the end of the century by the United States, which had previously been one of the largest borrowers. The development of the Third World did not begin until the last third of the nineteenth century when this flow of finance began to finance the railways, ports, and other infrastructure without which commerce could not move.

Although foreign capital was important to the Third World, the Third World in the nineteenth century was not all that important to foreign capitalists. In 1913 only about one-third of outstanding investment was in the Third World (excluding Argentina). The bulk of the investment was in Europe, North America, and the other temperate countries of recent settlement. Foreign investment and imperialism do not coincide.

It is particularly important to note that foreign investment was not based on the rich countries lending to the poor countries. Per capita income was higher in the United States or Australia or Argentina, which were borrowers, than it was in the United Kingdom, France, or Germany, which were lenders. If income per head were the chief determinant of self-sufficiency in finance, we could not answer the question posed by opponents of foreign aid: namely, if Britain and France were saving enough to be lending in the middle of the nineteenth century, when they were not much richer than Ceylon or Brazil is today, why cannot the developing countries now save for themselves all the capital they need?

In the nineteenth century the distinction between the European lenders and the rich borrowers turned on differences in rates of urbanization. Those whose urban populations were growing by less than 3 percent per annum (France 1.0, England 1.8, and Germany 2.5) loaned, and those whose urban populations were growing by more than 3 percent per annum (Australia 3.5, United States 3.7, Canada 3.9, Argentina 5.3) borrowed.

Urbanization is a decisive factor because it is so expensive. The difference between the costs of urban development and rural development does not turn on the difference of capital required for factories and that required for farms. Each of these in a small part of total investment, and the difference per head is not always in favor of industry. The difference turns on infrastructure. Urban housing is much more expensive than rural housing. The proportion of urban children for whom schooling is provided is always much higher, at the stage where less than 60 percent of children are in school. The town has to mobilize its own hospital service, piped water supplies, bus transportation. In all these respects the towns require more per head in terms of quantity than rural areas, but even if quantities per head were the same, urban facilities would cost more in money terms than rural facilities. Rural people do more for themselves with their own labor in such matters as building houses, or working communally on village roads or irrigation facilities. When they hire construction workers they pay less, both because of a generally lower price level and because they are not faced with powerful construction unions. Rural people also do not hire architects.

The cause of these high rates of urbanization has been population growth—in Europe in the nineteenth century and in the developing countries in the second half of the twentieth century. Rural people have to move when population starts to grow, because this menaces the family farm. The family farm can be passed on intact if about two and one-half children per family survive to age of reproduction, of the eight or so born into the average rural family. As the number of survivors increases, the farm is threatened with dismemberment unless some sons move out. If there is plenty of land, as in West Africa, they can move out to make new farms or to seek employment on other new or expanding farms. If there is little new, cultivable land, they look to the towns. They will not go to the towns unless employment is known to be expanding there. If there is no work in the towns, or on other farms, the sons stay on the family's farm, which is then cut up into smaller and smaller pieces in the way with which we are so familiar in Southern Asia and the Middle East.

Therefore, in countries where all the land that can be cultivated without great expense is already occupied, the natural increase in the rural population seeks employment in the towns, once economic development has begun. The quantitative significance of this migration depends on two factors, the rate of natural increase of the population and the already existing ratio of urban to total population. At the end of the nineteenth century, Germany's population was growing at about 1.2 percent per annum. The urban population was 48 percent of the whole. To absorb the whole increase, the urban population had to grow at a rate of 1.2 divided by 48, i.e. by 2.5 percent per annum, which is exactly what it was doing. By this time emigration from Germany had virtually ceased. In Latin America, the population increases at about 3 percent per annum, and the urban population is already about 50 percent, so to absorb the whole natural increase the towns would have to grow at 6 percent per annum. This also is just about what the Latin American towns are averaging; the rural population remains constant while all the natural increase is accumulating in the towns. Asia and Africa cannot reach this condition because, though their population growth rates are about the same as the Latin American or even lower, say 2½ percent, their current urbanization level is lower still, say about 20 percent, so if the towns were to take all the natural increase they would have to grow at 12½ percent a year, which is virtually impossible.

The evidence suggests that in a complex industrial system whose interdependent parts must grow in some sort of balance if profitability is to be retained, employment in manufacturing and mining cannot grow faster than about 4 percent per annum. Japan has the fastest growth rate, and its industrial employment grew in the 1960s only at 3.8 percent a year. The figure for the United States in its heyday before the First World War was 3.5 percent a year. The U.S.S.R. reached 4.6 percent per annum in the 1930s but was then producing mainly armaments and factories to make armaments, which is a relatively simple system; in the 1960s, industrial employment in the U.S.S.R. grew only at 2.5 percent a year. It looks as if a complex industrial system cannot expand employment at more than 4 percent a year.

The problem is not so acute in Africa, where there is still plenty of land, as it is in South Asia, where there is not. Given its population growth rates, South Asia needs both more cultivable land and also more employment in agriculture per acre. These are its two highest priorities. This is not just a matter of providing work, over and above what non-agricultural activity can reasonably be expected to provide. It is also a matter of providing food for an exploding population. But even with all that can be done to make more employment in agriculture, rapid urbanization remains inevitable.

Urbanization would not be inevitable if industry could be spread around the countryside instead of concentrating in towns. This has been a deliberate objective of Mao's China. There are, however, two limits to what is possible. One is that people will migrate to the towns if they are allowed to do so; hence a system of permits to reside in the town, ruthlessly enforced, is an integral part of such a policy. And, second, industry is itself gregarious; most industrialists prefer to establish themselves in existing industrial centers, which already have not only the requisite physical infrastructure but also the network of institutions that binds industrial establishments together. One can work hard at establishing rural industries, but except in police states, success is bound to be limited.

The financial dependence of the developing countries on the developed is not due to their poverty, since even the richest countries have been borrowers. Neither does it derive from their unwillingness to save. Net domestic saving of the developing countries averaged about 10 percent a year in the 1960s, which is not very different from the ratios of Britain or France in the 1860s, when they were already lenders and not borrowers.

The developing countries' dependence for finance derives ultimately from their high rates of population growth, and intermediately from their high rates of growth of urbanization—around 5 percent per annum and more—to which this population growth gives rise. Population growth has already started to diminish (urbanization seems to be the basic constraint on population growth), but the dependency on borrowing will probably continue until the rate of natural increase drops to about one percent per year. Thus, it is likely to be with us at least until the end of this century.

It should be noted that dependence on international borrowing and dependence on foreign entrepreneurship are not the same thing. Britain was still borrowing from the Dutch in the eighteenth century, though not using Dutch entrepreneurship. The importance of direct private investment in the international flow is always greatly exaggerated, both by those who oppose it and by those who believe that it should be the principal channel for foreign transfers. The current scope for direct foreign investment is rather small. Plantations, public utilities, and mines were the usual sectors for private foreign investment up to 1929. The investment in plantation companies, which was associated with the movement of Indian and Chinese labor across the world, ended after the First World War as that movement ceased, and the investment of foreign capital in agriculture is now almost zero. Investment in public utilities is also at an end. Part of the reason for this is that it has become the conventional wisdom that public utilities should be in the public sector, so the private utilities are being bought out one after another. In addition, inflation kills public utilities because their costs rise faster than their prices, which are usually subject to elaborate public control. No knowledgeable person would put private money into Third World public utilities today. In the 1950s and 1960s the unprecedented growth of world industrial production created a large demand for minerals, including oil, and this sector became a magnet for foreign private investment. However, its very profitability has killed it. One after another, the governments are buying out the mineral enterprises, usually at substantially less than their market value, so this sector will no longer attract much private foreign investment. The other profitable sector was the financial sector, including banking and insurance. This sector took money out of the developing countries, rather than putting money in, so the developing countries have been clamping down here as well.

As these traditional sectors for private foreign investment fade out, the new sector is manufacturing industry. It is at present a reluctant contributor; it is the only sector in which Third World governments are actively encouraging foreign investment, and they are finding fewer takers than they would like. Here the emphasis is not on finance but on technology and management. The share of manufacturing in gross investment is rather small, and, if it were only a question of money, most developing countries could finance their manufacturing sectors without foreign involvement. The foreigner contributes two things, a market connection and managerial expertise. He may also contribute technology, but in the standard light-industry factory the technology is well known, and one can purchase a new cement factory or a new textile factory virtually off the rack. Advanced technology is relevant only in a few highly sophisticated industries such as computers, motor cars, or petrochemicals, and these are of immediate interest only to large, already industrially sophisticated countries such as Brazil, Mexico, or India. Current discussion of international investment as if it were mainly a problem of handling multinational corporations is quite out of perspective.

The developing countries will depend on foreign borrowing long after they have ceased to depend on foreign enterprise.* One should note that the Communist countries are now among the biggest debtors, alleged to be owing the Western world some $32 billion. It is the fast pace of urbanization that makes a country short of capital rather than a dependence on managerial expertise.

---

* I have said nothing about the need of oil-importing LDCs to borrow money to finance their balance of payments deficits because this is a separate problem, so large and urgent in itself that an immediate solution has to be found, in the shape of medium-term loans from oil-producing countries to LDCs, through one channel or another. In this paper I confine myself to the relationships that developed over the century up to 1973 since these are likely to continue for some time.

8
INTERNATIONAL
FLUCTUATIONS

So much for the causes of financial dependence. I wish now to consider two disadvantages of this dependence that were already evident before the First World War. The first of these disadvantages is the vulnerability of debtors to international recession; the second is the speed with which the debt charges mount.

Exporters of primary products are vulnerable to international recession, whether they borrow or not, because the prices of their exports swing very widely over the course of the trade cycle. Various authors have sought to assess whether the degree of fluctuation was greater for agricultural or for industrial countries, using different definitions, and have reached different conclusions. The answer is not very important, for even if the fluctuations were equal, the agricultural countries could bear them less because their foreign exchange reserves are relatively smaller.

To the hazards inherent in the fluctuation of prices were added those of a simultaneous fluctuation in the flow of investment funds. This arose out of the miserly way Britain handled its adherence to the gold standard over the forty years before the First World War. The Bank of England kept very little gold—some say because gold yielded no interest, while others are more charitable. Whatever the reason, the consequence was that the Bank was forced to react to slight losses of gold, changing the Bank Rate an incredible number of times per year. Specifically, whenever Britain began to recover from cyclical recession there would come a point where the Bank began to lose gold, partly because the terms of trade would move adversely, and partly because international borrowers would temporarily withdraw gold to pay for purchases in other countries or at home. A financial crisis could occur, therefore, even before the trade cycle had reached its peak. The Bank Rate would go up sharply, and open market operations or their equivalent would be launched. At this point, overseas lending would be suspended because the stock exchange would react to the financial crisis, because the houses promoting such loans would think the moment inauspicious, and because those who held funds for foreign countries would keep them in London to earn the higher interest rates. So the borrowing countries were bereft of borrowing at the same time that prices moved against them.

Some of these stoppages were of long duration. The recessions of 1873, 1892, and 1929 turned into great depressions, with the final upturn into revival delayed for three or four years. Each of these recessions was marked by sharp declines in international investment. Borrowers could not meet their commitments, and a string of defaults (or as we would now call them "requests for rescheduling of debt") was inevitable. We tend to be shocked by such requests, but they are an old and intrinsic part of international investment. There was widespread defaulting in the 1820s, the 1840s, the 1870s, the 1890s, the 1930s, and the 1950s, and we are now waiting for the defaults of the end of the 1970s. The European capital market took such defaults in its stride. It knew that the borrowers would have to come back for more money, and could then be made to recognize outstanding obligations before becoming eligible for new borrowing. But the United States lost its temper when caught in the defaults of the 1930s, and with its "blue sky" laws, restricting the holding of foreign government bonds by financial intermediaries, effectively closed its long-term capital market to foreign governments, with unfortunate consequences for our day, which we shall discuss in a moment.

These great depressions with their long inroads into the flow of international investment were tied to what is now called the Kuznets cycle in the United States, which made the United States prosperous and depressed in alternate decades— prosperous in the 1880s, the 1900s, the 1920s, and the 1960s, and depressed in the 1870s, the 1890s, the 1930s, the 1950s, and the 1970s. Economists have forgotten the propensity of the U.S. economy to have these wide swings, with recession continuing for three or four years before a final upswing; and under the baleful influence of the National Bureau of Economic Research's three- to four-year reference cycles have come to believe that recessions usually last only 18 months. But this is quite unhistorical.

This shortness of memory has been aided by the fact that, not since the Second World War have we had a really great depression of the old-fashioned kind. The United States went into recession in 1970, had a half recovery to 1973, and collapsed again. The graph of industrial production looks very much like that of the downturn of 1892, followed by the little recovery to 1895, renewed decline, and the long uphill climb, which took another seven years to get back on trend, in 1902. As on previous occasions a deep slump in building lies at the core of this Kuznets cycle. But the 1970 fall was not as great as that of 1893 because of our new built-in supports; and the rest of the industrial countries did not join in the downturn until 1974. So what we are in now is only a pale reflection of the long and deep depressions that we used to get every twenty years or so.

Another kind of fluctuation affecting international investment was the long swing in prices that we now call the Kondratiev swing, after the great Russian economist who first identified it. The sharp fall in the price level that lasted from 1873 to 1895 bore heavily on debtors. Somewhat to our surprise, the flow of international investment was not interrupted by the adverse movement of the terms of trade that was built into it from 1880 onward, but the rise in the real burden of debt certainly played a role in the heavy defaults of the 1870s and the first half of the 1890s. This long downswing of agricultural prices repeated itself between the wars, and again in the 1950s and 1960s. Agricultural prices rose sharply at the time of the Korean war, and then dropped continually until the end of the 1960s, when they turned upward again. However, the downward movement of prices was relatively small after 1955; nothing like the downswings of 1873 to 1895, or of 1920 to 1938. Now we seem to have started another long upswing of prices associated again with relative agricultural shortage, and if it persists it will help to erode the real burden of the debts contracted in the 1950s and 1960s.

It is not possible to guarantee LDCs against the consequences of long and deep recessions of the Kuznets variety, though the maintenance of multilateral and bilateral government lending through such recessions is certainly an improvement on the past. Neither can we guarantee against long downswings of the general price level of the Kondratiev variety, even though the world now seems determinedly set on continual price inflation. But we should be able to navigate the short three- to four-year cycle which has occurred in the United States since about 1890 and which also has its own name, the Kitchin cycle, after the economist who identified it or, as some would say, who invented it and sold it to the National Bureau of Economic Research.

These cyclical fluctuations in trade and investment have played havoc with the agricultural countries because their effect was multiplied as it passed through to the domestic economy. As the flow of foreign funds dried up, domestic income fell by more than the original decline in foreign exchange. This could be mitigated by devaluation. During the long decline in prices from 1873 to 1895, those countries which remained on the silver standard, such as India, escaped internal deflation; India's prices actually rose throughout this period. Some other countries, such as Argentina, Chile, and Brazil, let their currencies float up and down. It paid the agricultural classes to let the peso fall as prices fell in gold. This kept up their incomes in pesos and, by preventing the urban community from enjoying the lower gold prices of industrial imports, also moved the terms of trade in favor of the agricultural classes. Those agricultural countries that clung to the gold standard, such as Australia and many European colonies, paid the penalty of sharp internal swings. The case of the United States is particularly interesting. The United States had been borrowing overseas through the 1880s, and was caught in a foreign exchange jam in the first half of the 1890s both because of the decline of British lending and because of the very low prices of its agricultural exports. Whether to remain on the gold standard became an acute political issue that was not settled until the second half of the 1890s by a combination of the election of 1896, the rise in prices of agricultural exports, and an explosion of exports of manufactures in the second half of the 1890s. Milton Friedman has concluded:

It should perhaps be noted explicitly that we do not intend to suggest that the alternative involving abandonment of the gold standard was economically undesirable. On the contrary, our own view is that it might well have been highly preferable to the generally depressed conditions of the 1890s. We rule it out only because, as it turned out, it was politically unacceptable.★

I think Professor Friedman must have changed his mind because, when lecturing in Israel in 1972 on the monetary problems of less developed countries, he advised that each such country should tie its currency to the currency of the country with which it did the most business, and just stay there.★★ He drew specific attention to the United States, which, he said, had thus "unified" the dollar with sterling at the end of the nineteenth century. In his 1972 view, this was an even better policy for a developing country than free floating.

There is in fact no easy path; this is a problem where every time you think about it you are liable to come to a different conclusion. Free floating is an obvious nuisance for countries with no organized forward markets. This is an important difference in the international economic order between the rich and the poor. But if an LDC maintains

★ Milton J. Friedman and Anna J. Schwartz, *A Monetary History of the United States 1875-1960*. Princeton, N.J., 1963: Princeton University Press, p. 111.

★★ Milton J. Friedman, *Money and Economic Development*. New York, 1973: Praeger Publishers, pp. 44-48.

fixed rates of exchange all through the cycle, it has to pay the cost of higher unemployment levels as external prices fall; also, even in the absence of cyclical phenomena, it must keep a tight rein on internal prices, lest it be priced out of its export markets. If on the other hand it is known to be ready to devalue whenever it runs into balance of payments problems, no one will be willing to hold its currency. The onset of every minor difficulty would lead to a rush to sell and an exhaustion of its foreign reserves. Besides, devaluation is a dangerous medicine for an economy whose imports are large relative to national income. This was not so in the nineteenth century, when food was a small part of Third World imports, and when trade unions had not yet acquired the power to keep real wages constant or rising in all situations. Nowadays such an economy is likely to find itself on a treadmill, where devaluation raises domestic money incomes and prices, so setting off further devaluation *ad infinitum*. Firm control over the money supply and over the level of money incomes is a pre-condition for successful floating, especially if food and other consumer goods are a large proportion of imports. Countries uncertain of their ability to pursue such policies will be reluctant to use the tool of devaluation, especially if the trouble in the foreign balance is thought to be temporary and cyclical.

What the situation requires is something the gold standard never had, namely a lender of last resort. France and Germany could ride the cycle up to 1913 because they kept huge hoards of gold. LDCs could not afford to do this. They could have afforded to hold larger foreign exchange reserves; but a debtor who holds large foreign exchange reserves is a man who is borrowing at 6 percent to keep money in the bank at 3 percent. Poor countries wish to avoid this. Britain avoided the same fate. Not only did she hold very little gold, borrowing from France and Germany in times of stringency as in 1890 and 1907, but instead of holding exchange reserves in other countries' banks, she relied on having other countries hold their reserves in sterling in her banks and on such reserves moving in and out at her convenience, as signaled by changes in Bank Rate. This system worked for Britain until 1931, when it broke down. It could never have worked for the less developed countries, since an LDC that raises its bank rate is signaling a crisis that is more likely to drive money out than to bring money in. We have to recognize that the instruments available to developed countries for controlling the flow of foreign exchange over the trade cycle are simply not available to the developing countries. This is another of the clefts in the international economic order.

By 1939 it was clear that the foundation of any new international monetary system must be a lender of last resort, and this was built into the International Monetary Fund. Such a system is not easy to operate, and the IMF has had to learn its business painfully as it went along. It sounds straightforward to have an agency that passes out money as industrial output in the developed countries declines and gets it back as industrial output revives. This part of the problem gave little trouble before 1973, since the cyclical movement was rather mild. IMF capacity to deal with it was also strengthened by setting up compensatory financing, to help developing countries whose exports have fallen off temporarily, and the EEC compensatory fund, which serves the same purpose for its African, Caribbean and Pacific (ACP) associated nations, will also help. So also will the proposed commodity buffer stocks scheme, if it gets off the ground.

But a lender of last resort is faced with many demands arising out of situations that are not so obviously self-correcting, and for which long-term finance is more appropriate than short-term lending. One country runs out of foreign exchange because it has experienced an unusual drought for three years running; how will it be able to pay back temporary lending? Another country is in trouble because some new synthetic has cut its export prices in half. Another country has used suppliers' credits excessively to finance long-term investment, and now cannot meet its debt charges. Yet another has been financing capital formation by inflation, and cannot face the unemployment that deflation will bring. The IMF faces two kinds of difficulties in dealing with such requests. One is where the deficit is due to the government's own policies, which the government refuses to change; this has led to the biggest quarrels. The other is where the appropriate remedy is not short- but long-term finance. To be a lender of last resort is not an enviable position, since one is inevitably faced with demands to which unrestricted short-term lending is not the appropriate answer. The availability of adequate long-term finance is a necessary condition for simplifying the role of short-term institutions.

THE VOLUME
OF DEBT

Let me now leave the problem of fluctuations and address the second big disadvantage of financial dependency, namely the speed with which the debt charges pile up.

Domar has given us the formula for the ratio of debt charges to new annual lending.★ It rises asymptotically to a limit

$$\frac{D}{F}L = \frac{a + i}{a + g}$$

where a is the annual repayment ratio (on the diminishing balance principle), i is the rate of interest, and g is the rate of growth of annual lending. Thus, if the rate of interest is 5 percent, and annual lending grows by 5 percent, the debt charge will mount until it exactly equals the annual lending. If lending is to contribute net resources to the borrower, it must grow faster than the rate of interest.

In the British case, in the last quarter of the nineteenth century lending grew less rapidly than the rate of interest. So from 1890 onward new lending was less than the sum of repayments, interest, and dividends. The average difference in

★ E. D. Domar, "Foreign Investment and the Balance of Payments," *American Economic Review*, December 1950.

favor of Britain was £42 million a year, from 1890 to 1907. Only in the final prewar spurt between 1908 and 1913 did average lending exceed the average inflow, and then only by an average of £3 million a year.

In consequence, the debt situation in 1913 was incredible. For comparison let us look at the situation of developing countries in 1972, just before the explosion of oil prices affected the situation. Outstanding debt of developing countries was then 1.8 times annual exports. (Government debt was $85 billion, private investment $53 billion, and exports $75 billion.) This ratio of 1.8 was already thought to be very high; people were worrying about it and calling for debt cancellation. By comparison, ratios of debt to exports (not debt charges but outstanding debt) were enormous in 1913. The lowest ratios, those for India, Japan, and China, were around 2¼. Australia's ratio was 4.8, Latin America's 5.2, and Canada's 8.6.

How does one meet debt charges on obligations that are 8.6 times exports? If the debt charge were 10 percent (say 5 for interest and 5 for repayment), it would absorb 86 percent of export proceeds. Argentina's debt charge in 1890 was 60 percent of her exports. Countries in this situation would certainly have been in trouble if they had been required to amortize their debts in cash. However, there is no such call. In the first place, part of this debt is not debt but equity in private corporations, which is not repatriated until it is sold to citizens of the debtor country. (Transnational corporations were already very much in evidence in 1913; the recent discovery of their existence by political theorists puzzles the historian a little.) But in any case, even the debt proper does not have to be diminished: it can be simply rolled over in one way or another, including the exchange of new debt for old.

This, it must be said, presupposes that new debt can be used to extinguish old debt. This is not so if the new debt is tied to specific projects and must therefore be used to finance new purchases of equipment and construction. The new debt of 1913 had an advantage over much of the debt of 1972, since in 1913 a government could borrow in London for unspecified purposes, or even specifically to pay off the old debt or the interest thereon; whereas in 1972 the World Bank and the bilateral government lenders were insisting on tying new loans to new projects.

In any case the volume of debt is of no significance if the loans have been invested economically. One may run into cyclical problems, but I am assuming that these are handled by a short-term lender of last resort. By "invested economically" I mean that the loan must add more to national income than it costs. But I also assume that the economy is able to translate extra income into foreign exchange: to convert it into tax revenues if the loan is for a public purpose, and to convert these revenues into foreign exchange. I also assume that enough of this extra income accrues within the lifetime of the loan, i.e. that one is not borrowing on short-term to finance long-term investment. Given these conditions, a loan is not a burden but a blessing; the larger the debt burden, the better off the country will be.

In practice the two assumptions most often violated in the last two decades have been convertibility into foreign exchange, and the use of short-term financing. Otherwise, real national income in the developing countries has been growing at 5 percent a year, so their capacity to absorb capital fruitfully is beyond dispute, as is also their ability to mobilize domestic resources for meeting long-term obligations, if they wish to do so.

Now in a neo-classical world there is no separate foreign exchange problem; domestic resources can always be translated into foreign exchange, given appropriate fiscal, monetary, and exchange rate policies. A large structuralist literature exists that discusses whether such policies may not at some times or in some places conflict with the larger requirements for sustaining economic growth or full employment, and I shall not enter into it at this time. Since this literature relates to the foreign exchange earning capacity of the developing countries, the figures are worth noting. Allowing for adverse terms of trade, the purchasing power of LDC exports increased at just under 5 percent per annum between 1955 and 1970, or roughly at the same rate as national output. Before the First World War, tropical exports grew faster than tropical output; exports were the engine of growth. Nowadays there is more production for the home market, and the developing economy's growth does not depend so much on having a rising ratio of exports to national income. All the same, the fit in the 1950s and 1960s was rather close; but whether it was just right or, if not, whether the villain was the failure of demand for traditional exports on the part of the industrial countries, or the failure of the LDCs to take advantage of the new possibilities offered by world trade in cereals, meat and manufactures is precisely what the argument is about.

To continue with the figures, in 1972 the ratio of debt charges to exports (including amortization, interest, and profits whether reinvested or not) was about 23 percent. This appears to be a large figure, but on the other side of the balance sheet the inward flow of grants, loans, and private investment, excluding technical assistance, was about 36 percent of exports, making an overall net inflow of about 13 percent of exports. This is a much healthier situation than existed in 1913 or in 1890. (It corresponds incidentally to a net inflow of 2.3 percent of national income, to be added to gross domestic savings then running at about 15 percent of national income. If we leave out interest and dividends and concentrate on the capital flow, the difference between loans and grants and repayments comes to a net inflow of about 4 percent of national income.)

These ratios of debt to exports are relevant only to the structuralist position, which implies that there is a maximum that the ratio of debt charges to exports should not be allowed to exceed, say 25 percent. Such an approach is unfair to the larger countries, which, because of their geographical diversity, import very little. India, for example, needs to import only about 5 percent of national income, and on any such rule of thumb is permitted a maximum debt charge of 1.7 percent of national income. The error in this approach is that it assumes that a country with relatively small imports must also have relatively small exports. But if India's debt charges came to 5 percent of national income, why should she not meet her obligations by importing 5 percent and exporting 10 percent of her national product? If debt limitations are to be imposed, they should be in terms of national income and not trade.

My point is that if the loans are economic, in the sense that they raise income by more than their cost, it should not matter how large is the accumulated debt—the more the merrier. One begins to worry if the income cannot be converted into foreign exchange, but here again one need not worry if the debt is being rolled over, or new debt used to extinguish old debt, as was obviously the case before the First World War. One would indeed expect a country to go through a sort of investment life cycle, in four stages. In stage one, new borrowing exceeds the debt charges; so even the interest is coming out of new borrowing. In stage two, new borrowing is less than the debt charge but more than the amortization. In stage three, the amount of outstanding debt is falling;

and in stage four, the country has become a net creditor. The developing countries as a group were still in stage one in 1972.

Why then did we hear so much in the 1950s and 1960s about the burden of debt, and why were there so many defaults? The answer lies mainly in the excessive proportion of short-term debt. In 1913 Britain's outstanding short-term loans were only about £300 million in contrast with £3,500 million at long-term. But the developing countries have been shut out of the long-term capital markets of Britain, France, and the United States by the foreign exchange restrictions of the first two and by the "blue sky" laws of the third. This exclusion of LDC governments from private portfolio borrowing is a major change in the international economic order, with major adverse consequences. Government-to-government lending is a partial but insufficient substitute. Therefore, LDC governments have been driven into short-term borrowing; through suppliers' credits in the 1950s and 1960s, and commercial bank loans in the first half of the 1970s.

The use of short-term suppliers' credits to finance long-term investment could of course only lead to default, as over a dozen countries discovered. Sometime in the 1960s it dawned on the industrial nations first that they were losing money, and second that with world trade in manufactures growing by 10 percent a year, this kind of aggressive competition to sell to people who could not repay was hardly necessary, so they began to clamp down on suppliers' credits.

Just as these controls began to be effective, the Eurocurrency market and the governments of the developing countries discovered each other. From the standpoint of a developing country, a Euro-bank is a wonderful institution. It takes two years to borrow from the World Bank, which rightly demands expensive feasibility studies, asks hundreds of questions, brings in large, time-consuming teams on innumerable visits, and issues mountains of paper, whereas one can borrow from a Eurobank in a few weeks, on the basis of conversations and letters. This flexibility has special value because it means that new borrowing can be used to repay old borrowing, which is one of the conditions required for a high debt ratio to be tolerable, when the loans are not repaying themselves. Then there is the wonderful banking practice of "rolling over," which seems to mean that the loan need never be repaid. So the developing countries have plunged into this market with zest, among the largest borrowers now being such governments as those of Brazil, Zaire, Mexico, and Indonesia.

Superficially this is a most precarious situation, and there is even fear that the inability of such governments to repay their loans may bring down the whole international banking system. But why should they be called on to repay? A banker lends money to earn interest. So long as the interest is safe, there is no need to repay the principal. The loan can be rolled over. A customer who insists on repaying is just a nuisance who is putting the banker to the trouble of finding another customer. But of course this interest is not safe. It is vulnerable to fluctuations in the borrowers' ability to earn foreign exchange. And if the interest becomes doubtful, the demand that the principal also be repaid at short notice could prove very troublesome.

What we need is an adequate flow of long-term finance, of various kinds, through all conceivable channels, including a long-term capital market reopened to good borrowers, supplemented by the multilateral and bilateral government agencies, and by private foreign investment, on terms ranging from market rates to grants to the poorest countries. This has been agreed by governments ever since the beginning of the 1960s. Members of the Organization for Economic Cooperation and Development (OECD) are pledged to an annual net flow of not less than one percent of their national incomes, and have further agreed that the average rate of interest on the government-to-government part of this flow should not exceed 3 percent. If the developed countries actually honored these commitments, which are not particularly burdensome, the flow of long-term finance on reasonable terms would be adequate (leaving aside the question of oil). We could reduce the short-term borrowing and would not have to bother about the burden of debt. The problem, then, is how to get the developed countries to keep their commitments, but this is outside my present terms of reference.

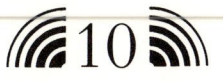

THE ENGINE
OF GROWTH

The final element of the international economic order that I wish to consider is the dependence of the developing countries on imports into the developed countries for their engine of growth. When the developed countries are expanding, as in the thirty years up to 1913, the developing countries move ahead; when the developed are depressed, as they were for the nearly three decades that included the two world wars, the developing are almost at a standstill. And when the developed revive and grow faster than ever, as between 1950 and 1973, the developing also grow faster than ever.

We even have a precise measure of the link. World trade in primary products grew about 0.87 times as fast as industrial production in the developed countries between 1883 and 1913, and again between 1951 and 1970. Insofar as exporting primary products is the engine of growth of the developing countries, this engine beats rather more slowly than industrial production. Actually the trade of the developing countries grows faster than this indicates, since it is not confined to primary products. Taking everything together, the ratio has been about one to one.

This sort of dependence is inconsistent with one of the objectives of the developing countries, namely that their per capita incomes should grow faster than those of the developed—that the gap between standards of living be narrowed, and ultimately eliminated. I think most people interested in international relations would welcome the narrowing of the gap, whether they are rich or poor. But let us consider the effects of the link. Theoretically, one of the simpler ways of narrowing the gap would be for the richer countries to grow less rapidly, as their environmentalists are urging them to do. But if the richer countries grow less rapidly, the poorer countries will grow less rapidly too, and will indeed get the worst of the bargain, since the terms of trade will move against them. Given the link, it is in the interest of the poor countries that the rich grow as fast as possible.

It is indeed one of the complaints of the poor countries that the rich do not buy enough from them: that the rich countries protect their own competing, high cost production, whether of sugar and fruit, or whether in the processing of raw materials, or in manufacturing. The elimination of these barriers to trade is one of the main demands in the charter for a new international economic order. Estimates of how much more the LDCs could then export start at $10 billion a year.

A low value for the link between industrial production and the demand for tropical products impedes the attainment of the growth targets that the United Nations has set for the developing world.

The target for the 1970s was 6 percent per annum. It was thought that this would require imports to grow by 6 or 7 percent per annum, and that exports should also grow by 6 or 7 percent per annum, keeping constant the ratio of the gap between imports and exports. But if industrial production in the rich countries grows only at 5.4 percent per annum, as it did in the 1950s and 1960s, imports of primary products will grow only at 4.7 percent, and cannot sustain the 6 percent growth target for the developing countries.

It is not surprising, therefore, that developing countries resent the dependence of their growth rate on what happens in developed countries and would like to be free.

Absolute freedom is not possible. Any country that exports is to that extent dependent on world trade. The issue therefore turns, first, on whether the developing countries are too dependent on exports of primary products and, second, given some dependence on exports, whether they could not do better exporting more to each other and relatively less to the developed countries.

We have already explored the origins of the excessive dependence of the LDCs on exporting primary products. This export was the easiest line to follow in the last quarter of the nineteenth century. However, it should have led, as in Australia or Canada, to the development of a domestic market that would serve as an additional engine of growth for industrial and agricultural production. It failed to do this adequately for a number of reasons, which we have also examined. There was no revolution in domestic food production, so LDCs became importers of food. Finance and trade in primary products were dominated by foreigners, who looked outward rather than inward. Those whose interests were bound up with growing and exporting agricultural products used their political power against industrialization. The factoral terms of trade were unfavorable, so the domestic market for manufactures was in any case rather small.

The picture has changed over the last twenty years. Political power, which was formerly used against industrialization, is now used in favor of industrialization. But the domestic market is still small, partly because the revolution in food production is only just beginning, and partly because the factoral terms of trade are still unfavorable. So industrialization has run through the domestic market rapidly, and its momentum has been saved only by the opening up of the rich countries to imports of manufactures from the poor.

When the LDCs switch from exporting primary products to exporting manufactures to the rich countries, they exchange one dependence for another. The potential scope is much wider. There is a limit to the amount of tea or cocoa or coffee that the rich countries will buy, but with exports of manufactures from LDCs standing only at 8 percent of world trade in manufactures in 1975, potentially unlimited growth is available in this area to LDCs over the next decade or so. World trade in manufactures has been growing by 10 percent per annum, and so have exports of manufactures from LDCs. If this pace continued, LDCs would merely be holding a constant proportionate share of world trade, and this should not present either party with insuperable difficulties. It is, however, unlikely that world trade in manufactures will grow indefinitely at 10 percent per annum, when world production of manufactures grows only at 5 to 6 percent per annum. If the growth rate now falls, LDCs will need an increasing share of world trade in manufactures, and, though this is not difficult for the next decade or so, it is bound to face increasing resistance.

The fact is that the LDCs should not have to be producing primarily for developed country markets. In the first place, they could trade more with each other, and be less dependent on the developed countries for trade. The LDCs have within themselves all that is required for growth. They have surpluses of fuel and of the principal minerals. They have enough land to feed themselves, if they cultivate it properly. They are capable of learning the skills of manufacturing, and of saving the capital required for modernization. Their development does not in the long run depend on the existence of the developed countries, and their potential for growth would be unaffected even if all the developed countries were to sink under the sea. I make the point only to remind ourselves that the current relationships are not among the permanent ordinances of nature; it is not intended as a recommendation.

If there is going to be an exception to this underlying independence, it will be in the area of food. Currently the LDCs have enough land to feed themselves if they cultivate it properly, but their populations are growing rapidly. If population overtakes food supply in Asia, the Asians will look to the rest of the world for cheap food. If this is not forthcoming they will almost certainly look for land. Three centuries ago North and South America, Australia, and Africa were more or less empty. The world's population was concentrated in Europe and Asia. The Europeans seized the two Americas and Australia, and commenced a rapid peopling of these continents, to the exclusion of Asians. They also taught the Asians how to bring about a population explosion. Now that the Asians have followed their example and doubled the rate of growth, they too need more space. This will not be a problem if the Asians quickly control their growth; or if agricultural technology improves even faster than we expect; or if Europe and the Americas can feed the Asians cheaply, and take Asian manufactures in return. Otherwise, the prospect for intercontinental peace in the twenty-first century is not good.

Even leaving aside the question of food, and leaving aside long-run considerations, there is a special sense in which some developing countries need current access to the markets for manufactures in the developed countries. We encourage the LDCs to form customs unions to enjoy the benefits of regional integration, especially in coordinating their industrial development. They have tried to do this and have produced a series of integration treaties, in Latin America, Central America, Andean America, West Africa, East Africa, and South East Asia, all of which are in deep trouble. The two main reasons are well known. First, each country wishes to produce for itself the whole range of light manufactures, so it is really only a few large-scale heavy industries that are in practice eligible for integration, and over these there is much quarreling. Second, in every region some countries are more advanced than others and benefit more from integration, at the expense of the others. So the agreement is unstable.

Actually, up and coming industrial nations do not depend on protection in the markets of impoverished neighbors. They go where the market is, namely in the rich countries. Thus when Germany erupted into world trade in manufactures in the 1880s, it was by flooding the British market; and when the United States took its turn at the end of the century, its biggest markets were in Europe, not in Latin America. The up and coming industrial nations of the next two decades, led by Brazil, Mexico, and India, are going to make their way primarily through trading with the richer countries rather than through trading with the poorer. The parceling of the world market into a set of regional enclaves has some merit if the developed countries close off their markets to the manufactures of developing countries. If they do not, the arrangement will not survive except where it is cemented by strong political considerations, as in Western Europe.

In any case the individual LDC does not have to be so dependent on exports in its development strategy. It should look more to the home market. What limits industrial production for the home market is the small agricultural surplus of that 50 percent or more of the labor market that is engaged in growing food for home consumption. Transform this mass of low level productivity, and the whole picture changes. The LDCs cease to have to import food, and instead penetrate the rising world market for cereals, beef, and feeding-stuffs. The factoral terms of trade move dramatically in favor of the traditional tropical agriculture crops, and the home market for industrial products and high level services becomes the engine of growth. These countries, upon becoming richer, would do absolutely more trade than they do at present, but it would be more varied, and would also be in smaller proportion to national income, if the import propensities of today's rich countries are any guide.

To summarize, international trade became an engine of growth in the nineteenth century, but this is not its proper role. The engine of growth should be technological change, with international trade serving as lubricating oil and not as fuel. The gateway to technological change is through agricultural and industrial revolutions, which are mutually dependent. International trade cannot substitute for technological change, so those who depend on it as their major hope are doomed to frustration. The most important item on the agenda of development is to transform the food sector, create agricultural surpluses to feed the urban population, and thereby create the domestic basis for industry and modern services. If we can make this domestic change, we shall automatically have a new international economic order.

POSTSCRIPT

The preceding lectures were historical and analytical, and therefore deliberately refrained from advocating solutions. However, readers who need solutions tend to read them into a text, and to attribute to the writer positions which he does not hold. In order to minimize misunderstanding, it may help to indicate briefly what the historical record seems to suggest as areas for improving economic relations between developed and developing countries.

1. The principal cause of the poverty of the developing countries, and of their poor factoral terms of trade is that half their labor force (more or less) produces food at very low productivity levels. This limits the domestic market for manufactures and services, keeps the propensity to import too high, reduces taxable capacity and savings, and provides goods and services for export on unfavorable terms. To alter this is the fundamental way to change LDC/MDC relations. But this takes time.

2. Meanwhile, LDCs need a more rapid rate of growth of exports, to pay for needed imports and to meet their debt obligations. MDCs should make more space for the LDCs in world trade, by reducing their barriers to LDC exports of man-

ufactures and agricultural products. This is the best and most effective way of helping the LDCs.

3. LDCs need much greater access to long-term finance. The current proportion of short-term finance is excessive and dangerous. This was so even before the price of oil exploded. The oil crisis should be handled with medium term instead of short-term credits.

4. The IMF needs larger standby resources to cope with cyclical recession. In 1976 the exports of oil-importing LDCs came to $118 billion, but their borrowing power in the Fund was only $13 billion, plus small amounts of SDRs and commodity compensation finance. In the absence of buffer stocks, the standby finance reserved for LDC's should not be less than half a year's exports.

5. Secular price decline, such as occurred for LDC exports in the 1950s and 1960s aggravates the problems of LDCs, by discouraging exports, moving the terms of trade unfavorably, and aggravating the burden of debt. More space for LDCs in world trade would help to support the prices of their exports. So also would price stabilization schemes, which would also benefit developed countries by dampening the spread of international recessions.

There are many other issues on the agenda for international discussion, e.g., multinational corporations, the cost of international transfers of technology, and voting power in international assemblies. The above are those which stand out from the historical record as the most urgent.

INDEX

LIBRARY OF CONGRESS CATALOGING
IN PUBLICATION DATA

Lewis, William Arthur, Sir, 1915–
   The evolution of the international economic order.

   (The Eliot Janeway lectures on historical economics in
honor of Joseph Schumpeter; 1977)
   Includes index.
   1. International economic relations—Addresses, es-
says, lectures.   I. Title.
HF1007.L68   382.1   77-15374
ISBN 0-691-04219-5
ISBN 0-691-00360-2 pbk.